Habitats of AFRICA

by Bernice Rappoport

Table of Contents

What do you think about when you think of Africa? Camels making their way across a sandy desert? Lions and elephants feeding on grassy plains? Monkeys swinging through trees?

Deserts, grasslands, and forests are all **habitats** of Africa. A habitat is where animals live. A habitat has food, water, and shelter the animals need to stay alive.

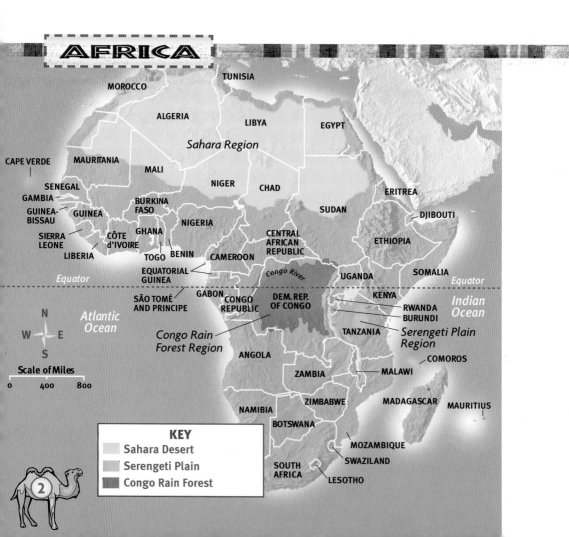

AFRICA

MOROCCO
TUNISIA
ALGERIA
LIBYA
EGYPT
Sahara Region
CAPE VERDE
MAURITANIA
MALI
SENEGAL
NIGER
CHAD
GAMBIA
BURKINA
FASO
ERITREA
GUINEA-
BISSAU
GUINEA
SUDAN
DJIBOUTI
NIGERIA
SIERRA
LEONE
CÔTE
d'IVOIRE
GHANA
CENTRAL
AFRICAN
REPUBLIC
ETHIOPIA
LIBERIA
TOGO BENIN
CAMEROON
Equator
EQUATORIAL
GUINEA
Congo River
UGANDA
SOMALIA
Equator
SÃO TOMÉ
AND PRINCIPE
GABON
CONGO
REPUBLIC
DEM. REP.
OF CONGO
KENYA
Indian
Ocean
N
Atlantic
Ocean
RWANDA
BURUNDI
W   E
Congo Rain
Forest Region
TANZANIA
Serengeti Plain
Region
S
ANGOLA
COMOROS
Scale of Miles
ZAMBIA
MALAWI
0   400   800
ZIMBABWE
MADAGASCAR
MAURITIUS
NAMIBIA
BOTSWANA
KEY
Sahara Desert
MOZAMBIQUE
Serengeti Plain
SOUTH
AFRICA
SWAZILAND
Congo Rain Forest
LESOTHO

The Sahara (suh-HAH-ruh) in Africa is a desert habitat. The Sahara is hot and dry. In many places it is very sandy. The Serengeti (sehr-un-GET-ee) Plain in Africa is a grassland habitat. It has large fields of grass. The Congo Rain Forest in Africa is a rain forest habitat. It is a wet, steamy place with thick plants, bushes, vines, and trees.

Get ready to take a trip to these habitats of Africa!

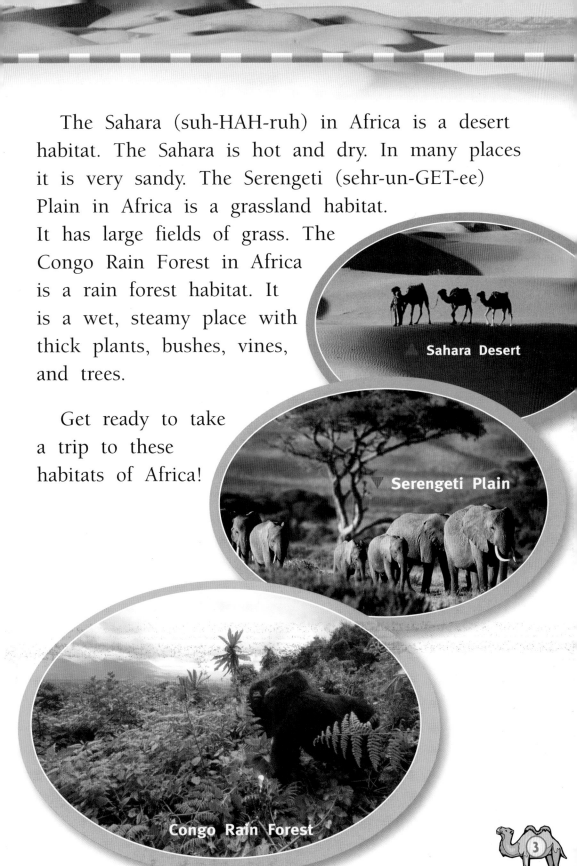

Sahara Desert

Serengeti Plain

Congo Rain Forest

The Sahara Desert

The Sahara is the world's largest desert. It is as large as the United States! The days are very hot and the nights are quite cold. Very little rain falls in the Sahara. Sometimes there is no rain for weeks and weeks.

Sandstorms happen a lot in this desert. Powerful winds blow the sand into mounds and hills, called **dunes**. The dunes change shape as the wind blows the sand.

The Sahara has large sand dunes.

Heat, cold, and dryness are all a part of the desert habitat. Desert animals have special ways to live with these different conditions.

Small animals protect themselves from the daylight sun. They dig a **burrow**, or hiding place. The burrow might be under a large rock or deep under the sand. When the temperature drops at night, the animals come out to search for food.

▲ Snakes hide under rocks or burrow in the sand to escape the burning sun.

▲ Scorpions hide under rocks during the day. At night, they catch spiders and insects.

▼ The Sahara has rocks and small bushes. The rocks and bushes make good hiding places for small animals and insects.

Desert animals can get water at an **oasis** (oh-AY-sihs). At an oasis, water comes from springs that are deep underground. Some water bubbles up above the ground and forms lakes.

An oasis also has trees. The most important trees are date palms. Their rich fruit is food for people as well as animals.

It's a Fact

Date palms can grow as tall as 100 feet (30 meters).

Dates on date palms grow in bunches. A single bunch can hold between 600 and 1,700 dates.

▼ Animals and people can live at an oasis.

The Camel

The camel's body helps it **survive,** or live, in the desert habitat. A camel can go for many days without food or water. When it does find water, the camel might drink up to fifty gallons at a time!

The fat in the hump can keep the camel alive when there is little food around.

Long eyelashes protect the camel's eyes from blowing sand.

The stomach can store enough water to last for two weeks.

Nostrils keep out the blowing sand.

Long hair protects the camel from sunburn. It keeps the camel's body warm at night.

Toes have loose skin between them. They keep the camel from sinking into the sand.

A **wadi** (WAH-dee) is another source of water for desert animals. It is a dry valley that collects water during the rainy season. The rain turns wadis into ponds and small rivers. Some of the rain soaks into the soil.

Small plants grow around a wadi. Animals come to eat these plants. But if a rainfall is heavy, some plants get washed away.

√**Point**

Reread
How are an oasis and a wadi alike? How are they different?

▲ Wadis provide water for desert animals and plants.

8

Most desert plants live on little water. Cold desert nights leave a wetness called dew. The leaves on some desert plants soak up the dew.

A little rain does fall in the desert. A plant with deep roots can get the water and store it for later use.

Everyday Science

Go outside in the early morning. Take a paper towel with you. Rub the towel on a few leaves. Check the towel to see whether it is wet from the dew.

▲ The leaves on this tree soak up the early morning dew.

The Serengeti Plain

The Serengeti Plain is part of the huge grassland areas in Africa. These areas are known as the **savanna**. The climate is warm, but not as hot as the desert.

Savanna lands are covered with tall grasses and a few trees. The trees provide shade and fruits. The savanna is a good habitat for many animals.

Two Trees of the Serengeti Plain

Two trees that are part of the grassland habitat are the acacia (uh-KAY-shuh) and the baobab (BAY-oh-bahb).

acacia

- It is called the "umbrella" tree.
- Its large branches give shade.
- Tall animals, such as the giraffe, feed on its leaves.
- The tree's fruit is food for animals. The fruit is a pod with seeds.

baobab

- Spiders, bees, and caterpillars live in this tree.
- The tree's fruit is called "monkey bread."
- Elephants and other animals eat the tree's leaves.
- Birds nest in the tree trunk and the branches.

The Serengeti Plain is home to many large animals. Most of them move in **herds**, or groups. Some herds are small and others can have hundreds of animals! The herds move from one feeding place to the next.

It's a Fact

Most of the Serengeti Plain is a national park. The government takes care of the land. Visitors to the park can take photographs. Park guides drive visitors around in buses.

▼ Wildebeests live on the Serengeti Plain.

Most animals stay with their herds. But as they move around the plain, some animals get too far away from the herd. These animals become **prey**. They become victims of an attack by another animal.

The attacking animal is called a **predator** (PREH-duh-tur). A predator quietly watches and waits. When an animal gets away from the herd, the predator springs into action.

▲ A lion attacks a zebra.

?Solve This

Being speedy is helpful for both predator and prey. Speed helps a predator catch its prey. Speed helps prey get away from the predator.

Look at the table below.
a. Which of the three animals is fastest?
b. Which animal is slowest?
c. In miles, how much faster is the ostrich than the lion?

Animals	Running Speed
lion 	35 mph (about 22 kph)
ostrich 	40 mph (about 25 kph)
zebra 	38 mph (about 24 kph)

Careers in Science: Naturalist

If you like animals, you might want to become a naturalist (NACH-uhr-uh-list). For this kind of work, you need a degree in biology, natural science, or education. Naturalists study the habits and needs of animals. They help people respect animals and their habitats.

a nature center

a zoo

a wildlife refuge

The Congo Rain Forest

The Congo Rain Forest has a **tropical** (TROP-uh-kuhl) climate. It is always rainy and hot. So lots of plants grow in the rain forest. That means lots of food for plant-eating animals.

The rain forest has different layers. The tree branches that block the sun are called a **canopy** (KAN-oh-pee). A canopy might be two hundred feet (about 61 meters) above the ground! The canopy, understory, and forest floor are home to different animals.

Gorillas in the Congo Rain Forest ▶

canopy

Birds, monkeys, and other small animals feast on fruits and leaves in the canopy.

understory

Lizards and small animals like rats and mice find food in the understory. This layer of the rain forest has small shade trees, bushes, and vines.

forest floor

Insects and other small creatures make their homes on the forest floor. This layer has small shade trees, bushes, and vines.

A Rain Forest Home

The rain forest is home to many apes. Apes live in trees or on the ground.

Gorillas are the largest apes. They live on the ground and feed on fruits, roots, and leaves.

Chimpanzees live in trees. They eat nuts, leaves, insects, and meat.

It's a Fact

An adult gorilla can grow to 600 pounds (about 272 kilograms).

▲ Chimpanzees are known as the smartest apes.

18

Jane Goodall spent years studying chimpanzees in Africa. She visited Africa and got a job there. Her job was to watch chimpanzees and take notes about them.

Goodall started "talking" with the chimps by making signs with her hands. She believed that the chimps understood her signs. She wrote many books about how chimps behave. She helped the world find out many things about chimpanzees.

Goodall discovered that chimps use tools. Chimps use a twig from a tree branch to poke a hole in a termite nest. Then they pull the stick out and lick up the tiny insects stuck on it!

A Rain Forest in Danger

The Congo Rain Forest is faced with problems. Loggers have cut down trees. Some of the cleared land has been taken over by farms and houses.

This loss of forest affects the animals. Part of their habitat is ruined. Some rain forest animals have become **endangered** (en-DAYN-jurd). This means they may not be able to survive.

▲ Gorillas are losing their rain forest home.

Another problem in the Congo Rain Forest is hunting. Some hunting is against the law. Killing endangered animals is against the law.

✓Point

Talk About It
What do you most remember about the Serengeti Plain and Congo Rain Forest? Share your thoughts with some classmates.

Conclusion

➤ Remember the camel? It lives in the Sahara Desert where there are hot days, cold nights, and very little water. What other animals live in the Sahara?

➤ Remember the lion? It lives in the wide grassland of the Serengeti Plain. What other animals live on the Serengeti Plain?

➤ Remember the monkeys? They live in the hot, wet Congo Rain Forest. What other animals live in the Congo Rain Forest?

Habitats

Habitat	Animals	Plants
Sahara		
Serengeti		
Congo Rain Forest		

Glossary

burrow   (BER-oh) a tunnel dug by an animal into soil or sand (page 5)

canopy   (KAN-oh-pee) the top layer in a rain forest (page 16)

dune   (DOON) a hill of sand (page 4)

endangered   (en-DAYN-jurd) in danger of no longer existing (page 20)

habitat   (HAB-uh-tat) a place where animals live that has the food, water, and shelter they need to stay alive (page 2)

herd   (HURD) a large group of animals (page 12)

oasis   (oh-AY-sihs) a desert area with an underground supply of water (page 6)

predator   (PREH-duh-tur) an animal that hunts for its food (page 13)

prey   (PRAY) an animal that is hunted and killed for food (page 13)

savanna   (suh-VAN-uh) a flat, grassy area with few trees (page 10)

survive   (SUHR-vive) live (page 7)

tropical   (TROP-uh-kuhl) a climate that is hot and rainy (page 16)

wadi   (WAH-dee) a watering place for animals in the desert (page 8)

Solve This

Answer Key

Page 14
a. The ostrich is fastest.
b. The lion is slowest.
c. The ostrich is 5 miles per hour faster than the lion.

Index